MW00781141

VE

TO THE UTTERMOST

DEVOTIONAL READINGS FOR HOLY WEEK FROM JOHN PIPER

Cover design and typesetting
Taylor Design Works

Now before the Feast of the Passover, when Jesus knew that his hour had come to depart out of this world to the Father, having loved his own who were in the world, he loved them to the end.

John 13:1

TABLE OF CONTENTS

EDITOR'S PREFACE

There's nothing intrinsically holy about particular days, but for most of church history Christians have set aside eight days between Palm Sunday and Easter Sunday for solemn focus (Romans 14:5–6). This string of days provides an annual interval for us to focus intently on the greatest events in human history, the acts of our Savior Jesus Christ. "Fix your gaze steadily on him," John Piper writes of Holy Week, "as he loves you to the uttermost."

That one word—*uttermost*—is loaded with significance. Jesus willingly died for his friends and endured unimaginable degrees of suffering to do so (John 13:1). To love *to the uttermost* is to love freely, without reserve or limit, and without flaw or failure. Love to the uttermost is unquenchable, unstoppable, and resolute. As we watch his arrest and trial and death unfold for eight days, we gaze on a Christ who begrudges no pain or reproach on his pathway to redeem lost sinners. This is the man who "humbled himself by becoming obedient to the point of death, even death on a cross" (Philippians 2:8). This is love *to the uttermost*.

As the story of Christ's death freshly hits our senses, we read of a Savior who exercises his own authority over death and promises to take up his own life in the end (John 10:18). "Anybody who makes a statement like that," Piper writes, "is either mentally deranged, or lying, or God." Everything is at stake in how we respond to those options. What are we to do with this Jesus who loves to the uttermost and tramples death?

Love to the Uttermost is a devotional spanning from Palm Sunday to Easter Sunday. It is comprised of eight excerpts (plus one prologue reading) selected from John Piper's vast 33-year writing and preaching ministry at Bethlehem Baptist Church in the Twin Cities. This devotional can be used for personal, family, or group devotions. It can serve anyone who seeks a steadied gaze to watch our Savior as he loves us *to the uttermost*.

Tony Reinke
Desiring God

Prologue

A VISION FOR HOLY WEEK

As I have tried to prepare my heart to meet Jesus in a special way on Palm Sunday and Maundy Thursday and Good Friday and Resurrection Day, a series of pictures has come back to my mind again and again. Let me try to describe the story for you.

A little lamb was born all wooly-white with skinny legs and a wet nose, pretty much like all the other little lambs. But as the lamb grew into a sheep, the other sheep began to notice a difference. This sheep had a strange lump on his forehead.

At first, they thought he'd been hit, but the lump never went down. Instead, a large pad of deep, white wool grew over the lump and made it very soft and firm. The lump might have stopped attracting attention except for the fact that this sheep began to use the lump on his head in very strange ways.

For one thing, the lump seemed to weigh down his head so that he always looked like he was bowing and showing reverence to some invisible king. Then he began to seek out other sheep that were sick or wounded. He would use the firm, soft lump on his forehead to help the weak onto their feet and to wipe away tears.

Whole flocks of sheep started to follow him around, but the goats laughed him to scorn. Sheep were disgusting enough, but a sheep with a queer lump on his forehead was more than they could take. They harassed him all the time and made up jokes and taunts: "How come you hang your wooly head? Your lump made out of woolen lead?" And it just infuriated them that he would walk away from them and keep on doing his quiet works of mercy.

So one day the goats surrounded him and rammed him with their horns until he died, and they left him alone in the field. But as he lay there, something very strange happened. He began to get bigger. The bloody wool fell away and revealed a sleek, white, horse-like hair. The soft pad of deep white wool dropped off his forehead and straight out of the merciful lump grew a mighty horn of crimson steel unlike any horn that has ever been or will be again.

And then, as if by command, the massive Unicorn leaped to his feet. His back stood eight feet above the ground. The muscles in his shoulders and neck were like marble. The tendons in his legs were like cables of iron. His head was no longer bowed, and when he looked to the right or to the left, the crimson horn slashed the air like a saber dipped in blood.

When the sheep saw him, they fell down and worshiped. He bowed and touched each one on the forehead with the tip of his horn, whispered something in their ear, and soared away into the sky. He hasn't been seen since.

That's the vision in my mind as I enter Holy Week. It's a

portrait of Jesus Christ painted by Isaiah under the inspiration of God and put on display by Matthew 12:18–21. Like every good work of art, this portrait has a purpose, and the purpose is to cause us to set our hope on Jesus Christ. And I am praying that this will happen in your life, because I know that everything else you set your hope on will let you down in the end. But if you hope in Jesus Christ, he will be honored in your life, and you will never regret it.

Palm Sunday

SEEING THE KING ON PALM SUNDAY

"Fear not, little flock, for it is your Father's good pleasure to give you the kingdom." (Luke 12:32)

Today is Palm Sunday. We picture ourselves welcoming the King into our city and into our hearts. He tries to make his intentions known by coming, not on a great stallion, but on a lowly donkey, meek and humble.

I wonder how many here look upon this lowly Servant-King and feel that this is just a thin veneer, and that beneath this lowly exterior there is a terrible power and authority which is just waiting to burst out against you if you slip in any way. I wonder how many feel that it is not really the deepest pleasure of this King's heart to serve his people and meet their needs.

I wonder how many feel that he's riding this donkey of lowliness as a kind of camouflage. And once he gains a foothold, he will throw off his rags, pull out his sword, and storm forth to do what he really loves to do, namely, judge and destroy. Of course, some will be saved—the few who somehow could please him. But that is not his heart's desire. He is basically angry—always angry. And the best we can do is stay out of his way, and maybe, if we keep the rules well enough, we could sneak by him when he is in one of his temporary good moods.

God's Deepest Delight

Jesus is at pains to help you *not* feel that way about God. And I want to draw your attention to one verse, namely, Luke 12:32, because every little piece of this verse is intended to help take away the fear that Jesus knows we struggle with, namely, that God begrudges his benefits, that he is constrained and out of character when he does nice things, that at bottom he is angry and loves to vent his anger.

Luke 12:32 is a verse about the nature of God. It's a verse about what kind of heart God has. It's a verse about what makes God glad—not merely about what God will do or what he has to do, but what he delights to do, what he loves to do, and what he takes pleasure in doing. "Fear not, little flock, for it is your Father's *good pleasure* to give you the kingdom."

The phrase "good pleasure," is a verb in Greek: "to be a pleasure" or "to be pleased by." You could translate it: "It pleased God," or, "God chose it gladly." In other words, God is not acting in this generous way in order to cloak and hide some malicious motive. The word "good pleasure" utterly rules that out. He is not saying inside, "I will have to be generous for a while even though I don't want to be, because what I really want to do is bring judgment on sinners."

The Lord's meaning is inescapable: God is acting here in freedom. He is not under constraint to do what he doesn't really want to do. At this very point, when he gives his flock the kingdom, he is acting out his deepest delight. This is what the word means: God's joy, his desire, his want and wish and hope and pleasure and gladness and delight, is to give the kingdom to his flock.

Monday

HE SET HIS FACE FOR JERUSALEM

> *When the days drew near for him to be taken up, he
> set his face to go to Jerusalem. And he sent messengers
> ahead of him, who went and entered a village of the
> Samaritans, to make preparations for him. But the
> people did not receive him, because his face was set
> toward Jerusalem. And when his disciples James and
> John saw it, they said, "Lord, do you want us to tell
> fire to come down from heaven and consume them?"
> But he turned and rebuked them. And they went on
> to another village. (Luke 9:51–56)*

In Luke 9:51–56, we learn how *not* to understand Palm
Sunday.

To set his face towards Jerusalem meant something very
different for Jesus than it did for the disciples. You can see
the visions of greatness that danced in their heads in verse
46: "An argument arose among them as to which of them
was the greatest." Jerusalem and glory were just around the
corner. O what it would mean when Jesus took the throne!

But Jesus had another vision in his head. One wonders how he carried it all alone and for so long.

Here's what Jerusalem meant for Jesus: "I must go on my way today and tomorrow and the day following, for it cannot be that a prophet should perish away from Jerusalem" (Luke 13:33). Jerusalem meant one thing for Jesus: certain death. Nor was he under any illusion of a quick and heroic death. He predicted in Luke 18:31–33: "See, we are going up to Jerusalem, and everything that is written about the Son of Man by the prophets will be accomplished. For he will be delivered over to the Gentiles and will be mocked and shamefully treated and spit upon. And after flogging him, they will kill him."

When Jesus set his face to go to Jerusalem, he set his face to die.

The Time Had Come

Remember, when you think of Jesus's resolution to die, that he had a nature like ours. He shrunk back from pain like we do. He would have enjoyed marriage and children and grandchildren and a long life and esteem in the community. He had a mother and brothers and sisters. He had special places in the mountains. To turn his back on all this, and set his face towards vicious whipping and beating and spitting and mocking and crucifixion, was not easy. It was *hard*.

We need to use our imagination to put ourselves back into his place and feel what he felt. I don't know of any other way for us to begin to know how much he loved us. "Greater love has no one than this, that someone lay down his life for his friends" (John 15:13).

If we were to look at Jesus's death merely as a result of a betrayer's deceit and the Sanhedrin's envy and Pilate's spinelessness and the soldiers' nails and spear, it might seem very involuntary. And the benefit of salvation that comes to us who believe might be viewed as God's way of making a virtue out of a necessity. But once you read Luke 9:51, all such thoughts vanish.

Jesus was not accidentally entangled in a web of injustice. The saving benefits of his death for sinners were not an afterthought. God planned it all out of infinite love to sinners like us, and he appointed a time.

Jesus, who was the very embodiment of his Father's love for sinners, saw that the time had come and set his face to fulfill his mission: to die in Jerusalem for our sake. "No one takes my life from me," Jesus said, "I lay it down of my own accord" (John 10:18).

Tuesday

DEPTH OF LOVE FOR US

While we were still weak, at the right time Christ died for the ungodly. For one will scarcely die for a righteous person—though perhaps for a good person one would dare even to die—but God shows his love for us in that while we were still sinners, Christ died for us. (Romans 5:6–8)

As I have pondered the love of Christ for us, and the different ways that the Bible presents it to us, I have seen four ways that the depth of Christ's love is revealed.

First, we know the depth of someone's love for us by what it costs him. If he sacrifices his life for us, it assures us of deeper love than if he only sacrifices a few bruises. So we will see the depth of Christ's love by the greatness of what it cost him.

Second, we know the depth of someone's love for us by how little we deserve it. If we have treated him well all our life, and have done all that he expects of us, then when he loves us, it will not prove as much love as it would if he loved us when we had offended him, and shunned him, and disdained him. The more undeserving we are, the more amazing and deep is his love for us. So we will see the depth of Christ's love in relation to how undeserving are the objects of his love (Romans 5:5–8).

Third, we know the depth of someone's love for us by the greatness of the benefits we receive in being loved. If we are helped to pass an exam, we will feel loved in one way. If we are helped to get a job, we will feel loved another way. If we are helped to escape from an oppressive captivity and given freedom for the rest of our life, we will feel loved another way. And if we are rescued from eternal torment and given a place in the presence of God with fullness of joy and pleasures forevermore, we will know a depth of love that surpasses all others (1 John 3:1–3). So we will see the depth of Christ's love by the greatness of the benefits we receive in being loved by him.

Fourth, we know the depth of someone's love for us by the freedom with which they love us. If a person does good things for us because someone is making him, when he doesn't really want to, then we don't think the love is very deep. *Love is deep in proportion to its liberty.* So if an insurance company pays you $40,000 because you lose your spouse, you don't usually marvel at how much this company loves you. There were legal constraints. But if your Sunday School class makes all your meals for a month after your spouse dies, and someone calls you every day, and visits you every week, then you call it love, because they don't have to do this. It is free and willing. So we will see the depth of Christ's love for us in his freedom: "No one takes my life from me; I lay it down of my own accord" (John 10:18).

To push this truth to the limit, let me quote for you a psalm that the New Testament applies to Jesus (Hebrews 10:9). It refers to his coming into the world to offer himself as a sacrifice for sin: "I delight to do your will, O my God" (Psalm 40:8). The ultimate freedom is joy. He rejoiced to do his redeeming work for us. The physical pain of the cross did not become physical pleasure. But Jesus was sustained through it all by joy. He really, really wanted to save us. To gather for himself a happy, holy, praising people. He displayed his love like a husband yearning for a beloved bride (Ephesians 5:25–33).

WHY JESUS IS ALL-TRUSTWORTHY

"I am telling you this now, before it takes place, that when it does take place you may believe that I am he." (John 13:19)

Jesus himself taught that all the prophecies about him would be fulfilled. In other words, we have a testimony, not only that the writers themselves saw Jesus's life as fulfillment of prophecy, but that Jesus did, too.

For example, in Luke 22:37, Jesus says, "I tell you that this Scripture must be fulfilled in me: 'And he was numbered with the transgressors.' For what is written about me has its fulfillment" (see Isaiah 53:12). Jesus saw that the predictions of the Messiah and his sufferings would be fulfilled in himself.

Jesus took up the principle of John 13:19 and foretold numerous details of what was going to happen to him so that we might believe when they happened. "He began to teach them that the Son of Man must suffer many things and be rejected by the elders and the chief priests and the scribes and be killed, and after three days rise again" (Mark 8:31). Jesus saw the predictions of the Messiah and his sufferings being fulfilled in himself.

> He foresaw that his death would be by crucifixion (John 3:14; 12:32).

> He predicted that the disciples would find an unridden colt when they entered the town (Luke 19:30).

> When the disciples entered Jerusalem that last Thursday, he predicted they would meet a man with the water pitcher who would have a room for them to meet in (Luke 22:10).

> After three years of waiting, he knew the exact hour of his departure out of the world (John 13:1).

> Jesus knew that he would be betrayed, and who would betray him, and when it would happen (John 6:64; 13:1; Matthew 26:2, 21).

> He knew and predicted the fact and the time of Peter's three denials (Matthew 26:34).

> Jesus predicted that the disciples would all fall away and be scattered (Matthew 26:31; John 16:32; Zechariah 13:7).

> Jesus prophesied that he would be "lifted up from the earth" (John 12:32). That is, he would not be stoned but crucified—not by Jews but by Romans. So the decisions of Pilate and the Jews of how to dispose of him were a fulfillment of his prediction.

He makes all these predictions, according to John 13:19, so that we would believe he is God, that what he says about himself is true.

In other words, Jesus is saying, "If you are struggling to believe that I am the promised Messiah, that I am the one who was in the beginning with God and was God (John 1:1), that I am the divine Son of God, who can forgive all your sins and give you eternal life and guide you on the path to heaven, then I want to help you believe. And one of the ways I am going to help you have well-grounded faith is by telling you what is going to happen to me before it happens, so that when it happens, you will have good reason to believe in me."

THURSDAY OF THE COMMANDMENT

> *"A new commandment I give to you, that you love one another: just as I have loved you, you also are to love one another." (John 13:34)*

Today is Maundy Thursday. The name comes from the Latin *mandatum*, the first word in the Latin rendering of John 13:34, "A new commandment (*mandatum novum*) I give to you, that you love one another: just as I have loved you, you also are to love one another." This commandment was given by Jesus on the Thursday before his crucifixion. So Maundy Thursday is the "Thursday of the Commandment."

This is *the* commandment: "love one another: just as I have loved you." But what about Galatians 5:14? "For the whole law is fulfilled in one word: 'You shall love your neighbor *as yourself*.'" If the whole law is fulfilled in "Love your neighbor *as yourself*," what more can "Love one another *as Christ loved you*" add to the fulfillment of the whole law?

I would say that Jesus did not replace or change the commandment, "Love your neighbor *as you love yourself*." He filled it out and gave it clear illustration. He is saying,

> *Here is what I mean by "as yourself." Watch me. I mean: Just as you would want someone to set you free from certain death, so you should set them free from certain death. That is how I am now loving you. My suffering and death is what I mean by 'as yourself.' You want life. Live to give others life. At any cost.*

So John says, "By this we know love, that he laid down his life for us, and we ought to lay down our lives for the brothers" (1 John 3:16). Was Jesus loving us "*as he loved himself*"? Listen to Ephesians 5:29–30, "No one ever hated his own flesh, but nourishes and cherishes it, just as Christ does the church, *because we are members of his body*."

In the horrors of his suffering, Christ was sustained "by the joy that was set before him" (Hebrews 12:2). And that joy was the everlasting gladness of his redeemed people, satisfied in the presence of the risen king.

Therefore, let us see the greatest love in action on Maundy Thursday and tomorrow on Good Friday. "Having loved his own who were in the world, he loved them to the end" (John 13:1). He loved us to the uttermost. And let us be so moved by this love that it becomes our own. "He laid down his life for us, and we ought to lay down our lives for the brothers." This is *the* commandment. This is *the* Thursday.

WHAT GOOD FRIDAY IS ALL ABOUT

> *Consequently, he [Jesus] is able to save to the*
> *uttermost those who draw near to God through him,*
> *since he always lives to make intercession for them.*
> *(Hebrews 7:25)*

The great passion of the writer of Hebrews is that we "draw near" to God (Hebrews 4:16; 7:25; 10:22; 11:6). Draw near to his throne to find all the help we need. Draw near to him, confident that he will reward us with all that he is for us in Jesus. And this is clearly what he means in Hebrews 10:22, because verse 19 says that we have confidence "to enter the holy place," that is, the new heavenly "holy of holies," like that inner room in the old tabernacle of the Old Testament where the high priest met with God once a year, and where his glory descended on the ark of the covenant.

So the one command, the one exhortation, that we are given in Hebrews 10:19–22 is to draw near to God. The great aim of this writer is that we get near God, that we have fellowship with him, that we not settle for a Christian life at a distance from God, that God not be a distant thought, but a near and present reality, that we experience what the old Puritans called communion with God.

This drawing near is not a physical act. It's not building a tower of Babel, by your achievements, to get to heaven. It's not necessarily going into a church building, or walking to an altar at the front. It is an invisible act of the heart. You can do it while standing absolutely still, or while lying in a hospital bed, or while sitting in a pew listening to a sermon.

Drawing near is not moving from one place to another. It is a directing of the heart into the presence of God who is as distant as the holy of holies in heaven, and yet as near as the door of faith. He is commanding us to come, to approach him, to draw near to him.

The Center of the Gospel

In fact, this is the very heart of the entire New Testament gospel, isn't it? That Christ came into the world to make a way for us to come to God without being consumed in our sin by his holiness.

› "For Christ also suffered once for sins, the righteous for the unrighteous, that he might bring us to God" (1 Peter 3:18).

› "For through him [Christ] we both have access in one Spirit to the Father" (Ephesians 2:18).

› "We also rejoice in God through our Lord Jesus Christ, through whom we have now received reconciliation" (Romans 5:11).

This is the center of the gospel—this is what the Garden of Gethsemane and Good Friday are all about—that God has done astonishing and costly things to draw us near. He has sent his Son to suffer and to die so that through him we might draw near. It's all so that we might draw near. And all of this is for our joy and for his glory.

He does not need us. If we stay away he is not impoverished. He does not need us in order to be happy in the fellowship of the Trinity. But he magnifies his mercy by giving us free access through his Son, in spite of our sin, to the one Reality that can satisfy us completely and forever, namely, himself. "You make known to me the path of life; in your presence there is fullness of joy; at your right hand are pleasures forevermore" (Psalm 16:11).

Saturday

A HOLY WEEK VOLCANO

Now the men who were holding Jesus in custody were mocking him as they beat him. They also blindfolded him and kept asking him, "Prophesy! Who is it that struck you?" And they said many other things against him, blaspheming him. (Luke 22:63–65)

As I read these terrible words, I found myself saying to Jesus, "I'm sorry. I'm sorry, Jesus. Forgive me!" I felt myself to be an actor here, not just a spectator. I was so much a part of that ugly gang that I knew I was as guilty as they were. I felt that if the rage of God should spill over onto those soldiers and sweep me away, too, justice would have been done. I wasn't there, but their sin was my sin. It would not have been unjust for me to fall under their sentence.

Has it ever bothered you that sometimes in the Old Testament when one man sins, many get swept away in the punishment God brings? For example, when David sinned by taking a census of the people (2 Samuel 24:10), "there died of the people from Dan to Beersheba 70,000 men"

(2 Samuel 24:15). In another example, Achan kept some of the booty from Jericho and his whole family was stoned (Joshua 7:25). Maybe my experience in reading Luke 22 is a clue to the divine justice in this.

My Volcanic Rebellion

An analogy came to my mind. The hearts of humanity are like a molten mantle beneath the surface of the whole earth. The molten lava beneath the earth is the universal wickedness of the human heart—the rebellion against God and the selfishness toward people. Here and there a volcano of rebellion bursts forth which God sees fit to judge immediately. He may do so by causing the scorching, destructive lava to flow not only down the mountain which erupted, but also across the valleys which did not erupt, but which have the same molten lava of sin beneath the surface.

The reason I confess the sin of beating Jesus, even though I wasn't there, is that the same lava of rebellion is in my own heart. I have seen enough of it to know. So even though it does not burst forth in such a volcanic atrocity as the crucifixion, it is still deserving of judgment. If God had chosen to rain the lava of their evil back on their own heads and some of it consumed even me, I would not be able to fault God's justice.

We may wonder why God chooses to recompense some evils immediately and not others. And we may wonder how he decides whom to sweep away in the judgment. Why seventy thousand? Why not fifty thousand, or one hundred, or ten? Why Achan's wife and not the greedy neighbor two tents down? I doubt that answers are available to us now. We are left to trust that these decisions come from a Wisdom so great that it can discern all possible effects in all possible times and places and people. How widely the lava of one person's rebellion and judgment will flow lies in God's hands alone.

And I believe from Romans 8:28 that, even though the lava of recompense overtakes me at a distance from the volcano, there is mercy in it. I do not deserve to escape, for I know my own heart. But I trust Christ, and so I know the judgment will be turned to joy. Though he slay me, yet will I trust him. For precious in the sight of the Lord is the death of his saints.

SUCH AMAZING RESURRECTION LOVE

> *"For this reason the Father loves me, because I lay down my life that I may take it up again. No one takes it from me, but I lay it down of my own accord. I have authority to lay it down, and I have authority to take it up again. This charge I have received from my Father." (John 10:17–18)*

Why does Jesus say this? Why does he stress his willingness to die? Because if it weren't true—if his death were forced on him, if it weren't free, if his heart weren't really in it—then a big question mark would be put over his love for us.

The depth of his love is in its freedom. If he didn't die for us willingly—if he didn't choose the suffering and embrace it—then how deep is his love, really? So he stresses it. He makes it explicit. *It comes out of me, not out of circumstances, not out of pressure, but out of what I really long to do.*

Jesus is stressing to us that his love for us is free. He seems to hear some enemy slander saying, "Jesus doesn't really love you. He's a mercenary. He's in it for some other reason than love. He's under some kind of constraint or external compulsion. He doesn't really want to die for you. He's just got himself somehow into this job and has to submit to the forces controlling him." Jesus seems to hear something like that, or anticipate it. And he responds, "No one takes it from me, but I lay it down of my own accord. I have authority to lay it down, and I have authority to take it up again." So he is pressing this on us to see if we will believe his protest of love, or if we will believe the opposite—that his heart is really not in this.

Anybody who makes a statement like that is either mentally deranged, or lying, or God. *I have authority from inside death, as a dead man, to take life back again, when I please.* Now what's the point here? Well, which is harder: to control when you die, or to give yourself life again once you are dead? Which is harder: to say, "I lay my life down on my own initiative"? Or to say, "I will take my life back again after I am dead"?

The answer is obvious. And that's the point. If Jesus could—and did—take his life back again from the dead, then he was free indeed. If he controlled when he came out of the grave, he certainly controlled when he went into the grave.

So here's the point. The resurrection of Jesus is given to us as the confirmation or evidence that he was indeed free in laying down his life. And so the resurrection is Christ's testimony to the freedom of his love.

The Meaning of Easter

Of all the great things that Easter means, it also means this: it is a mighty "I meant it!" behind Christ's death. I meant it! I was free. You see how free I am? You see how much power and authority I have? I was able to avoid it. I have power to take up my life out of the grave. And could I not, then, have devastated my enemies and escaped the cross?

My resurrection is a shout over my love for my sheep: It was free! It was free! I chose it. I embraced it. I was not caught. I was not cornered. Nothing can constrain me to do what I do not choose to do. I had power to take my life from death. And I have taken my life from death. How much more, then, could I have kept my life from death!

I am alive to show you that I really loved you. I freely loved you. Nobody forced me to it. And I am now alive to spend eternity loving you with omnipotent resurrection love forever and ever.

Come to me, all you sinners who need a Savior. And I will forgive you and accept you and love you with all my heart forevermore.

⽸ desiringGod

The mission of Desiring God is that people everywhere would understand and embrace the truth that God is most glorified in us when we are most satisfied in him. Our primary strategy for accomplishing this mission is through a maximally useful website that houses over thirty years of John Piper's preaching and teaching, including translations into more than 40 languages. This is all available free of charge, thanks to our generous ministry partners. If you would like to further explore the vision of Desiring God, we encourage you to visit www.desiringGod.org.

Desiring God

Post Office Box 2901, Minneapolis, Minnesota 55402
888.346.4700   mail@desiringGod.org

Made in the USA
Coppell, TX
17 March 2022

75072466R00028